Private Railways in Hawke's Bay

By A. C. BELLAMY

NEW ZEALAND

The New Zealand Railway and Locomotive Society Inc.,
P.O. Box 5134, Wellington

Printed in New Zealand by Apex Print Limited,
52 Hutt Road, Petone

Distributed to the trade in New Zealand by Brick Row Publishing Co. Ltd. P.O. Box 33-449, Takapuna, Auckland, and in Australia by Beta Books Pty Ltd, 7 Northcote Road, Hornsby, New South Wales 2077.

ABOVE: A log hauler (at right) and horse tram working in the Umutaoroa area west of Matamau. This view gives an indication of the method used for arranging turnouts on wooden tramways.

From an illustration published in the Auckland Weekly News in 1913, A. C. Bellamy Collection

ON THE COVER: From 1925 to 1971 two small steam locomotives built by John Fowler and Company, Leeds, England, were used by the Napier Harbour Board, with other locomotives, for shunting the wharves and to assist with the construction of the breakwater. The Board numbered them 5 and 6. Here is No. 5, Fowler's No. 16342 of 1925, photographed at the port in March 1960.

Photograph: B. D. Whebell

Introduction

THIS booklet was first published in April 1962. At that time it was intended to be a guide to railway enthusiasts of the private railways that have existed in the Hawke's Bay area. Since that date, more research has been carried out and, although just what horse-drawn tramways were used in the bush, particularly in the early days, has been difficult to ascertain, a list is included later in this booklet. Lines that have used locomotives are included in the first section of the booklet, and are shown in geographical order. The writer would be grateful for any further information that readers may have regarding the lines included, and also any that may have been omitted.

Acknowledgements

I wish to acknowledge the use of material, for the preparation of this booklet, from the Napier Harbour Board; the Marine Department, Wellington (now the Marine Division of the Ministry of Transport); Borthwick C. W. S. (N.Z.) Ltd, Waingawa; and from Messrs W. W. Stewart, F. J. Neill, L. R. Young, G. C. Stewart, J. Edgar, A. K. Thomson and T. Crabtree. The contributions from members of the Hawke's Bay Branch of the New Zealand Railway and Locomotive Society, including D. W. Pryor and A. B. Fordyce, are also welcomed.

BIBLIOGRAPHY

Bayliss, W. *Takapau — the Sovereign Years, 1876-1976.*
Cassells, K. R. *The Sanson Tramway.*
McGregor, Miriam. *Early Sheep Stations of Hawke's Bay.*
Mooney, Kay. *History of the County of Hawke's Bay.*
Munro, R. S. *A Short Survey of the History of the Taradale District.*
Playle, F. O., Editor. *101 Years of Ormondville.*
Stewart, G. C. *End of the Penny Section.*

Newspapers

Hawke's Bay Herald, October 1885, February 1896.
Waipawa Mail, January and March 1885.

Unpublished Papers

Miscellaneous papers of H. S. Tiffen *et al* in the Hawke's Bay Museum and Art Gallery collection.
Notes of the late Major Wilson, from the diaries of F. Craron, Dannevirke.

PACIFIC FREEZING (NZ) LTD, ORINGI

THESE works were opened on 26 November 1981, just to the east of the Oringi railway station, whence the northern backshunt was extended under the overbridge on S.H.2 to provide a line into the works. Drewry "Dsa" 227 (latterly DSA320) was sold to the firm by the NZR, and this locomotive is used to shunt over two kilometres of works sidings, and in transfer duties between the works and the NZR yard at Oringi.

TAMAKI SAWMILLING COMPANY, TAHORAITI

THIS company was granted a private siding from the NZR station at Tahoraiti in April 1885, and built a tramline two miles in length into the Umutaoroa forest. It was reported that the steam engine to work the tramway had arrived by March 1885. The locomotive used was an ex-Wellington Steam Tramway motor which had been built by Messrs. Merryweather & Sons of London, being their No. 64 of 1877. The Company seems to have ceased operations in this area about 1897, and subsequently, in 1902, the tramway motor was sold to the Napier Harbour Board.

MANSON & COMPANY, TIKOKINO

THIS Company's mill was situated at Tikokino, inland to the northwest of Waipawa, and had no physical connection with New Zealand Railways. The mill was established in November 1904, and at that time was one of the largest in Hawke's Bay. There were more than four miles of tramway leading from the mill to the bush, over which a converted traction engine hauled the logs. The traction engine that was converted to rail operation was built by Burrell and Co. of Thetford, England, and was their No. 2418 built in 1901. This Company's operations were transferred to Te Kinga on the West Coast of the South Island in 1910.

The converted Burrell traction engine on Manson and Company's tramway at Tikokino about 1904. (From the A. C. Bellamy Collection)

PRIVATE RAILWAYS

This ex-NZR "A" class locomotive No. 193 (Dubs 655/1873) was photographed when it was the Gear Meat Company's No. 1, some time before its sale in 1915 to Thos. Borthwick and Sons Ltd at Pakipaki. (From the Russell Orr Studios Collection)

THOS. BORTHWICK & SONS (N.Z.) LIMITED, PAKIPAKI

THE Company's freezing works were situated at the north end of the Pakipaki station yard, and were connected to the NZR tracks by a private line which crossed the main highway. The private siding right was granted in November 1904, although the first recorded locomotive owned by the Company was ex-NZR "A" 193, an 0-4-0T purchased from the Gear Meat Company, Petone, in November 1914. This locomotive was in use until 1931. Another locomotive, an 0-6-0T Barclay, builder's No. 1197/1909 was purchased in 1929 from the Sanson Tramway. A new boiler was required for this locomotive, and was on order from the makers, Andrew Barclay & Sons, Kilmarnock, Scotland, at the time of the Napier earthquake. When the works were destroyed by this event

in February 1931, it was decided not to rebuild, and the railway was abandoned, although the new boiler was fitted to the locomotive before it was transferred to Waingawa, near Masterton.

Subsequently, in 1955, after several years of idleness, this locomotive was converted to diesel propulsion using a gearbox purchased from N.Z. Refrigerating Co., Imlay, Wanganui, and a 130-horsepower (96kW) engine, General Motors model No. 4082 with a Delco-Remy starter. The transmission incorporated an Andrews & Beaven right-angle reduction drive with output shaft on both sides, driving through duplex chain drive to the rear axle. The original coupling rods provided power to the other axles. This reduction gearing was removed in 1972 and was replaced by a new gearbox from David Brown

In 1929 Borthwicks purchased, for use at Pakipaki, a Barclay 0-6-0 tank locomotive (maker's No. 1197/1909) named Manawatu *from the Sanson Tramway. It was transferred to the Waingawa works near Masterton after the Pakipaki works were destroyed in the February 1931 Napier earthquake.*

From the W. W. Stewart Collection

Ltd, England, this being fitted by A. & G. Price Ltd at a cost of £10,000.

In maintenance overhauls over several years, various modifications have been made to the gearbox, clutch, and brakes, either by the Works Staff or by A. & G. Price, and to ancillary units by Clyde Engineering and other firms. Today, the only recognisable parts of the Barclay 0-6-0 which once served on the Sanson Tramway and at Borthwick's Pakipaki works, are the frames, wheels and coupling rods. To outward appearances, the locomotive which shunts Borthwick's Waingawa works in 1984 is a neat little diesel, and a blast from the air horn which once graced a Wairarapa railcar (or "Tin Hare" as they were known locally) merely enhances the image.

The formation of the private siding to the works at Pakipaki can still be seen, as well as the point where the level crossing existed across S.H.2 just north of the station.

NELSON BROS. LTD, TOMOANA

THE actual date of the opening of the Tomoana freezing works siding is not known, but it must have been about 1881 because, for the year ended 31 March 1882, the revenue in and out of the siding, then known as Nelson Bros. and Williams, was £593. The first export of frozen meat from Hawke's Bay was railed to the old Napier port on 3 April 1884 for shipping on the *Turakina*. Early in the 1890s, the Company had eight bogie freezer wagons of class "V" built by New Zealand Railways. These wagons carried the firm's name on the side and were taken over by the Railways Department in 1915, being numbered "V" 172 to 179 inclusive. Some lasted into the 1970s.

The Company's first locomotive was "A" 220, an 0-4-0T purchased from New Zealand Railways in 1891 for £500. "A" 220 was built by Dubs and Company of Glasgow in 1873, their No. 654. The "A" locomotive was out of service by 1898, and was later sold to the Nelson Harbour Board. In 1925 it was in the possession of Ellis & Burnand Ltd, of Ongarue, having passed through the hands of three owners in the intervening period.

The next locomotive purchased by Nelson Brothers was "D" 222, obtained from New Zealand Railways in 1915. It is presumed that

ABOVE: This ex-NZR "C" class 0-4-2 saddle-tank locomotive No. 194, later No. 505 in the Public Works Department's list and named Huki, was purchased by Nelson Brothers from the PWD in 1946 for use at Tomoana. It was originally built by Neilson and Company, Glasgow, maker's No. 1771, in 1873. (Photograph: G. W. Jenkinson)

BELOW: This Bagnall 0-6-0 tank locomotive was the works engine at Tomoana from 1933 to 1979, having been built in England in 1932, maker's No. 2475. It is still (1984) retained as a standby locomotive. (Photograph: I. Malloch)

from 1898 to 1915 the siding was worked by NZR locomotives to do the heavy shunting, while draught horses were used for lining up wagons in the works. The "D" locomotive, a 15-ton 2-4-0T built in 1880 by Neilson and Company, Glasgow, their No. 2566, remained in use from 1915 until the present steam locomotive was put into service in 1933.

This locomotive is an 0-6-0T built by Messrs. W. G. Bagnall and Company of Stafford, England, and was their No. 2475 of 1932. Although no longer used, the locomotive still has a current boiler certificate and is officially on standby. It has been steamed, under an arrangement with the works management who have given approval for up to six steamings annually on Company sidings, and indeed it was in use on 4 February 1984 running a shuttle service between Ellwood Rd., and Frederick St., on NZR sidings on the occasion of the Hastings Centennial celebrations.

Nelson Brothers also purchased from the Public Works Department, in 1946, an ex-NZR

ABOVE: The ex-NZR "D" class 2-4-0 tank locomotive No. 222 (Neilson 2566 of 1880) shunting livestock wagons at Tomoana about 1919. (From the A. C. Bellamy Collection)

BELOW: Ex-NZR "Tr" class diesel shunting tractor No. 23 (Drewry 2126 of 1939) was purchased by Nelsons in 1981 and was photographed at Tomoana on 1 June 1983. (Photograph: P. F. Dyer)

locomotive, "C" 194, bearing the name *Huki* and numbered 505 in the Public Works list. This 0-4-2ST locomotive had been built by Neilson & Company of Glasgow in 1873, and was their No. 1771. It had been used between 1919 and 1941 on the construction of the railway line to Gisborne, and on other work in the Gisborne area and at Ohakea. Earlier it had been used on railway construction in North Auckland. Although purchased as a standby locomotive, the boiler was found to be in a bad condition and an attempt was made to convert it to a diesel unit, using a Gardner motor recovered from a trawler wrecked at Portland Island off Mahia Peninsula. The conversion employed chain drive, but was not successful and the locomotive was ultimately scrapped in the 1950s.

In October 1979 the Bagnall steam locomotive was replaced by diesel shunters, first by "Tr" 116 on hire from New Zealand Railways, and later in March 1981 by two 75 kW "Tr" class 0-6-0 locomotives purchased from the Railways. "Tr" 23 (Drewry No. 2126 of 1939) has been repainted in works colours (buff), but "Tr" 25 (Drewry No. 2127 of 1939) is currently (1984) still in NZR livery, and is held as spare.

ABOVE: From 1923 to 1960, this ex-NZR "D" class 2-4-0 tank locomotive No. 576 (originally No. 170) was the works shunter at Whakatu. It was built by Neilson and Company, Glasgow, in 1880, maker's No. 2563.

Photograph: I. Malloch

HAWKE'S BAY FARMERS MEAT COMPANY LIMITED, WHAKATU

THE Hawke's Bay Farmers Meat Co. Ltd was granted a private siding from the NZR main line at Whakatu from 1 April 1914, although it was 1923 before they purchased their first locomotive. This was "D" 576 purchased from

the Stores Branch of New Zealand Railways at Mamaku. This 2-4-0T locomotive had originally been numbered "D" 170, and was built by Neilson and Company of Glasgow in 1880, being their No. 2563. Before delivery to Whakatu, a new boiler was built by A. & G. Price Ltd, Thames. This locomotive remained in service until July 1960, when it was replaced by a new diesel locomotive built by Messrs. A. & G. Price Ltd, their No. 197. This 13-ton diesel-hydraulic locomotive is powered by a Gardner engine, and is rated at 84.5 horsepower. It also features exhaust-gas cleaning equipment.

"D" 170 has been preserved by Mr Roger Redward. It was displayed at MOTAT in Auckland until 1975, when it was taken south to Christchurch for restoration.

The H. B. Farmers Meat Co. Ltd's Whakatu works were extended in 1975 and new sidings, opened on 30 January 1976, were laid to the east of the main line to serve the new cool stores. These are shunted by NZR locomotives or by a road tractor.

The new H. B. F. works at Takapau, opened on 12 November 1981, has sidings connected to the NZR, but these are shunted by road tractor.

ABOVE: In 1960, A. & G. Price Ltd, Thames, supplied this 13-ton diesel-hydraulic shunting locomotive to the Hawke's Bay Farmers Meat Company for use at Whakatu. It was photographed there on 1 June 1983.

Photograph: P. F. Dyer

The Ruston-Hornsby diesel-electric locomotive (No. 349083/1954) and the Drewry diesel (No. 2507/1954) at Awatoto in early 1964. (Photograph: T. Crabtree)

EAST COAST FARMERS FERTILIZER COMPANY, AWATOTO

THESE works, about six kilometres south of Napier, were built to supply the Hawke's Bay, Gisborne and Wairarapa areas with fertilizer, which was previously supplied from Aramoho near Wanganui. The Company's extensive sidings were opened in 1954.

For the opening of the plant, the Company purchased a new diesel locomotive, an 0-4-0 of 107 horsepower supplied by the Drewry Car Company of London, England, being their No. 2507 of 1954. In October 1964, a diesel-electric locomotive was purchased from the Timaru Harbour Board. This locomotive was built by Ruston & Hornsby, being their No. 349083 of 1954, and is still in service (1984). Carrying the name *Orbell*, it is their DE165 class, 165 horse-power (123 kW) diesel-electric locomotive. It uses crown wheel and pinion drive to the rear axle with coupling rods from the rear to the other two axles. It is capable of lifting 1000-ton loads out of the works sidings.

It is of interest to note that this locomotive was towed to Picton and crossed Cook Strait on the *Aramoana*. Due to difficulties with lubrication and failure of axlebox bearings under tow in the South Island, it was finally driven north under its own power on 20 December 1963 at its top speed of approximately 17 m.p.h. (27 km/hr).

Upon arrival of this locomotive at Awatoto, the Drewry locomotive was sold, and left on 29 April 1964 for Thames for an overhaul at A. & G. Price Ltd before being sent to the Northland Fertilizer Works at Whangarei.

During periods of overhaul, the Company has hired Fowler No. 5 from the Napier Harbour Board, "Tr" 105 ex-NZR at Waipawa, "Tr" 15, or sometimes a "Dsa" locomotive manned by NZR staff.

The Company also owned three old NZR passenger cars which were used for the storage of fertilizer around the works. These cars were later scrapped, some of their woodwork being salvaged for the repair of the former Wellington and Manawatu Railway Company carriage maintained by the New Zealand Railway and Locomotive Society's Hawke's Bay Branch at Clive.

NAPIER HARBOUR BOARD, NAPIER
("Hawke's Bay Harbour Board" as from 1 October 1975)

THE Napier Harbour Board was incorporated in the year 1875. Construction work on the breakwater commenced in 1886, and it was then that the Board purchased its first locomotive from New Zealand Railways. It was "A" 41 (Napier section numbering), previously "A" 70 (Hurunui-Bluff section numbering) whence it had been transferred in 1883.

The Harbour Board originally worked the line from the Ahuriri station to the breakwater, and the tramline for the construction of the breakwater. During the period they operated the line from the exchange sidings at Ahuriri, the Harbour Board ran regular trains for goods to and from the wharves and Cranby's siding. The locomotive roster was quite complicated so that operations did not clash, but in the main, in the latter years, one of the Fowlers was on general duties, the "Wa" worked the meat ships, while the other Fowler handled wagons for other shipping. The "Wa" 2-6-2T was a familiar engine to the Harbour Board's drivers, because even before its purchase in 1946, it had frequently been hired from the NZR as the occasion warranted.

That portion of the line from Ahuriri to the wharves was taken over by New Zealand Railways and operated by them as from 4 February 1957.

The tramline on the breakwater was physically connected to the NZR, but in 1962 it was not possible for the locomotive to run on to NZR tracks as two steam cranes used for lifting concrete blocks straddled the lines. Consequently, when No. 6 was overhauled to replace No. 5 locomotive, these engines had to be lifted to and from the NZR line by one of the steam cranes. It is of interest to note that from 1913 to 1931 there were three level crossings of the Harbour Board line with the 3ft. 6in. gauge Napier Electric

RIGHT, UPPER: The Napier Harbour Board's locomotive No. 6 (Fowler 16343 of 1925) hauling a load of goods from Ahuriri to the Port of Napier.

RIGHT LOWER: The Napier Harbour Board's locomotive No. 6, now preserved at the Tokomaru Steam Engine Museum between Palmerston North and Shannon, and, in the background, the ex-NZR "Wa" class 2-6-2 tank locomotive No. 220.

BELOW: The NHB's locomotive No. 5 (Fowler 16342 of 1925) on work train duties at the port in the 1950s.

From the W. W. Stewart Collection

PRIVATE RAILWAYS

ABOVE: The Napier Harbour Board's locomotive No. 1 (Dubs No. 649 of 1873) purchased from the NZR in 1886, where it had been the Napier Section's "A-41" since 1883 and before that "A" 70 in the South Island. (From the A. C. Bellamy Collection)

LEFT: A Merryweather steam tram motor of 1878, named Zealandia, in Lambton Quay, Wellington. One of these motors, purchased from the Tamaki Sawmilling Company, Tahoraiti, became the Napier Harbour Board's No. 2. (From a Burton Brothers photograph courtesy the National Museum and R. J. Meyer)

Tramways, and there is one recorded collision between a tram and a locomotive.

During the years of operation of their line, the Board owned the following locomotives:

Harbour Board No.	N.Z.R. Number	Dates Owned	Builder	Builders Number	Date
1	A 41	1886 -1925	Dubs & Co.	649	1873
2	—	1902 -1922	Merryweather	64	1877
3	—	1909 -1940	Scott Bros.	—	1909
4	D 195	1919 -1931	Neilson & Co.	1846	1874
5	—	1925 -1971	Fowler	16342	1925
6	—	1925 -1971	Fowler	16343	1925
7	F 230	1933 -1946	Dubs & Co.	1364	1880
—	Wa 220	1946 -1956	N.Z.R.	14	1896

RIGHT, UPPER: The ex-NZR "Wa" class 2-6-2 tank locomotive No. 220, built at the Addington workshops in 1896, was owned by the Napier Harbour Board from 1946 to 1956. (Photograph: T. Crabtree)

RIGHT, LOWER: The Scott "D", originally built in 1909 for the Napier Harbour Board, as converted (unsuccessfully) to a petrol-engined locomotive after the original boiler wore out, photographed at Napier Port on 24 September 1952. (Photograph: N.Z. Railways Publicity)

No. 2 was an ex-Wellington steam tram, and was purchased from the Tamaki Sawmilling Co. at Tahoraiti.

No. 3 was built by Scott Bros. of Christchurch, and was of the same design as the NZR's class "D" 2-4-0T. This locomotive was later converted by the NHB to a petrol locomotive, being fitted with a Thornycroft petrol engine. It was in use in this form for about two years, and could haul only one block truck to the breakwater.

Nos. 5 and 6, both 0-4-0T Fowler locomotives, were purchased new by the Harbour Board. The Board originally ordered 0-4-2T locomotives, but accepted John Fowler & Sons' tender for 0-4-0T locomotives as they were of a standard type, and at a more satisfactory price. These locomotives could haul 238 tons on level track. No. 5 is held for restoration by the Silver Stream Railway near Wellington, while No. 6 is in working order at the Tokomaru Steam Museum at Tokomaru, a short distance south of Palmerston North.

No. 7 was sold to Messrs. Ellis & Burnand Ltd at Mangapehi in 1946, and is now displayed in a park at Hamilton.

The 37-ton 2-6-2T "Wa" 220, purchased in 1946, began to give trouble in 1955 and was cut up in 1956. Its remains were shipped to England as part of a consignment of scrap in the *Antrim*.

At various times, the Harbour Board hired locomotives from the NZR. These included "Wa" 68, "Wa" 165, "Wa" 220, "Ww" 481 and "Ww" 679.

A Harbour Board report for 1945 showed that, at that time, they also owned 25 "M" wagons, 39 side-tipping wagons and 14 end-tipping wagons. Many of these wagons could be seen in later years stacked up at the Marine Parade end of the harbour works.

ROBERT HOLT & SONS LTD, TAWA SIDING, NAPIER

THE Tawa Timber Company (later Robt. Holt & Sons) opened a mill on this site at Waitane in Napier in 1959. A private siding connecting with the main line of the NZR between Napier and Westshore was opened in August 1959. Logs arrived daily from Kotemaori, and a small rail tractor was provided to shunt the wagons of logs under the gantry. This locomotive was locally made. It had a diesel motor of 51.8 b.h.p. at 1600 r.p.m. and weighed approximately 10 tons. The locomotive was mounted on a bogie from a Napier electric tram, which was also of 3ft. 6in. gauge.

The mill and locomotive are no longer in use, but a locomotive body minus the bogie, was moved to the Arthur Miller school in Taradale in August 1981, while the bogie is believed to have gone to MOTAT in Auckland.

ABOVE: Built on a bogie from an old Napier electric tramcar, this 10-ton diesel locomotive was used by the Tawa Company at Waitane in Napier from 1959.

Photograph: H. G. Aldrich

ROBERT HOLT & SONS LTD, PUKETITIRI

THIS company operated a sawmill in the Puketitiri area, north-west of Napier, from 1911 to 1940. There was a tramway on which horses and oxen were used until 1937 when a rail tractor was purchased. After the closing of the mill, the tractor lay idle for about two years. It was then transferred to the Ohurakura mill on the Napier-Taupo highway near Te Pohue, north of Napier.

It is understood that the rail tractor was purchased from the Federal Engineering Works, Wellington, who were agents for the "Haula" eight-wheel-drive rail tractor, which was based on the chassis of a Fordson tractor.

ROBERT HOLT & SONS LTD, OHURAKURA

THIS sawmill, situated on the Napier-Taupo road near Te Pohue, was operated from 1923 to 1960. The company had a tramway on which two rail tractors were used, the first being a Fordson 26-horsepower tractor built by Rail Tractors Ltd, Wellington, in 1929 and fitted with Nattrass patent drive. The second rail tractor, from the Puketitiri mill mentioned above, arrived in 1942. Upon the closure of the mill in 1960, the locomotives came back to the Napier yard and were presumably scrapped.

C. F. PULLEY, WAIROA

IN the *Hawke's Bay Daily Mail* Supplement of 1 July 1939, issued at the time of the opening of the railway to Wairoa, it was stated in some historical notes that a Mr Withel had "suggested to build a light railway from Waikokopu to Wairoa using the rails over the Te Uhi hills, just then discarded by the Wairoa flaxmill people. With the rails being very light, the track could be better described as a tramway."

Other than this quotation from the early part of this century, little else is known of this private railway, although it was in operation from 1912 until 1915 to serve a flaxmill. The rails were very light and apparently ran over the Te Uhi hill. The locomotive used on this line was a small 0-4-0 built by Black Hawthorn Ltd, being their No. 885 of 1887. It had been purchased second-hand from H. Brown of Inglewood, and was sold about 1915 to the Kauri Timber Co. at Auckland. In later years it was acquired by Ellis and Burnand, and was presumably used at their Manunui mill.

ABOVE: This little steam locomotive, supplied by Black, Hawthorn
and Company (maker's No. 885) to
H. Brown of Inglewood in 1887, was
sold to C. F. Pulley of Wairoa; about
1915 it was sold again, to the Kauri
Timber Company at Auckland, and
later it was at Ellis and Burnand's mill
at Manunui. (Photograph courtesy
R. W. Brown and F. K. Roberts)

RIGHT: The Union Foundry tractor
owned by Swifts (N. Z.) Ltd at
Wairoa. (From the A. C. Bellamy
Collection)

SWIFTS (NZ) LIMITED, WAIROA
(Now Waitaki-NZR)

DURING the construction of the Wairoa to Waikokopu Railway by the Public Works Department in 1923, a siding was laid into the freezing works a short distance east of Wairoa. From this time until the linking up of this line in 1938 with the railway being built northward from Napier, meat from these works was railed to Waikokopu and shipped from that port. During this period, the siding was worked by the Public Works Department, and from early photographs it appears that the meat was loaded into insulated boxes on "M" wagons.

On 25 January 1938, Messrs Swifts (NZ) Ltd took delivery of a rail tractor built by the Union Foundry at Stratford, being their No. 25. Originally this tractor had a chain drive to all four wheels, and a petrol engine, but when this wore out, a Fordson Major diesel engine was substituted with a locally-built gearbox added to provide reversing capability. This tractor is still in use, although it was re-engined for a second time in 1970 with a more powerful Ford engine. Four forward and four reverse gears work through a torque converter with the facility to lock the differential when extra power is called for. Working on the private siding, which is 1½ kilometres long, this locomotive can shift a load of 300 tonnes.

It is of interest to note that Swift's siding forms part of a triangle, and was the only place in the Wellington District where the 88-seat articulated railcars could be turned. This siding crosses the main road at Wairoa and, after a crossing accident, it was fitted with crossing lights which are worked by the tractor driver.

Shunting meat containers on the Waikokopu wharf, east of Wairoa, in the 1920s when the PWD was working this section of railway. The locomotive is a Simplex petrol-engined machine. (Photograph courtesy Mrs Ostler and R. J. Meyer)

PRIVATE RAILWAYS

THOMAS BROS., WAIKAREMOANA

LEFT: This massive timber trestle on Thomas Brothers' timber tramway in the Tuai region near Lake Waikaremoana is believed to have been the largest bush tramway viaduct ever erected in New Zealand. Sixty thousand feet of sawn timber were used in its construction. For the legs, 18-foot stays were used, all held together by nails, while above the creek bed, logs straddled three spans well "tommed" and tied to the legs that carried the deck. This structure, built by the sawmill staff under the direction of the Manager, carried the heaviest of logs. It was 365 feet (111 metres) long and carried the rails 80 feet (24.4 metres) above the creek bed. This photograph was probably taken about 1929 because the firm's Fordson rail tractor, acquired in 1928, is posed on the centre of the structure with two large logs in tow. The sawmill was sold in June 1939 by Captain D. V. Thomas to Mr H. N. Wilson, who continued to operate it.

From the A. C. Bellamy Collection

THIS firm in 1928 purchased a sawmill near Tuai from the Public Works Department, who had used the mill to cut timber for their construction work in the Tuai area. A sawmill had originally been operated in the region as early as 1916 by a Mr G. S. Ridley, but it was burnt down in 1919. Another mill was erected on a new site where it remained throughout the sawmilling operations.

When Thomas Bros. purchased the mill in 1928, horses were still being used to bring in the logs. A Fordson rail tractor was then purchased. This machine was connected by a drive-shaft to a separate bogie, the power being provided by the tractor, with each unit driving its four wheels by chains. Jack Golding was the driver, and the tractor proved an excellent machine with little maintenance considering the work it had to do. It was found that on bends on the wooden tram track, while the smaller weights of logs gave little difficulty, it was necessary to put light steel rails on the curves for the heavier logs, some of which were 60 feet or more in length.

The trams were taken right up into the bush, which created much construction work with cuttings and bridges, the method used being pick and shovel with a wheelbarrow. Bridges used a considerable quantity of timber, the largest bridge built being 80 feet (24.4 metres) above the creek bed and 365 feet (111 metres) long.

MISCELLANEOUS TRAMWAYS

WITH the extension of the railway southwards from Waipukurau in the 1880s, the rails entered the area known as the Seventy Mile Bush, which gave the opportunity for milling the timber in the area. Many sawmills were established, particularly in the area from Ormondville to Oringi, and many of these mills operated tramways. Most of these had wooden rails and were worked by horses. A number of photographs have been located of some of the tramways in the area, but details of the owners are not always known. However it is known that the tramways listed below were in existence at one time or another.

In the *Waipawa Mail* of 7 March 1885, there is an account of an accident on a horse tramway leading to a railway siding at Papatu, which was about one mile north of Ormondville. A child who had fallen asleep between the rails was hit by a logging trolley.

In 1876, when Waipukurau was the terminus of the railway being built southwards from Napier, a wooden tramway was apparently constructed from Waipukurau to Kopua. South of Takapau this followed a line to the west of the present road. H. Wilding leased 7000 acres of bush at Whenuahou which had been purchased by William Nelson in 1883 to obtain matai firewood for the freezing works at Tomoana, and Wilding established sidings at two and five miles south of Takapau on this tramway which was still in existence in 1884.

ABOVE: *This view of logs being hauled up the incline on Gamman and Company's tramway at Otanga, near Dannevirke, about 1907, gives a good impression of the character of typical bush and timber trams of the period.*

From the A. C. Bellamy Collection

Palmerston North Sash & Door Co.

In 1896 this company had a mill, known as the Hawke's Bay Sawmill, cutting timber about two miles west of Tahoraiti, the timber being transported by tramline to the Tahoraiti station yard.

In 1899 this company installed a mill alongside what is known as Grainger's Road, Kiritaki. The output was conveyed by tram to the Oringi station, a distance of six miles.

W. I. Irvine, Ruaroa, Tamaki River

Mr Irvine operated a sawmill on the banks of the Tamaki river about six miles from Dannevirke. The timber was conveyed by tram along Laws Road to the railway siding at Tapuata, south of Dannevirke.

Richter Nannestad & Co., Tamaki River

In 1886 this company's mill was situated at the edge of the bush on the western bank of the Tamaki stream, about one mile from the railway siding. In September 1886, the company was procuring iron rails to construct a substantial tramway to the siding. It was reported that there was an incline on the line enough for the loaded trucks to run down to the siding without any motive power other than gravity.

Gamman & Co., Dannevirke

Gamman & Co. were granted rights on 1 April 1901 to lay a tramway on railway land, and to erect an overbridge at 37 miles 78¾ chains near Piripiri.

G. A. Gamman & Co., Dannevirke

A lease was granted to this firm on 1 April 1899 to run a tramway under a railway bridge at Kopua.

Gamman & Simmonds, Tahoraiti and Otanga

In 1900 this company had a mill at Tahoraiti, but this was later moved to the Otanga flat north of Dannevirke. In a Government report for 1907, there is a photograph of a wooden tramway showing logging trucks being hauled up a steep incline by cable.

Geo. Wratt & M. Anderson, Dannevirke

In 1895 these gentlemen had a mill about one mile from Dannevirke on the Weber Road, where they cut totara from the Tepapakuku Block. The logs were transported to the mill by a tramline across the Mangatera River and alongside Millers Road to the mill.

Totara Sawmill Co., Dannevirke

This company was granted a lease on 1 January 1901 for the privilege of laying a tramway on railway land at Oringi.

W. F. Greenway, Dannevirke

Mr Greenway was granted the privilege of tramway access at Victoria station (latterly Papatawa, now closed) from 1 April 1901.

Luxford & Wylde, Ngapaeruru

This company operated a wooden tramway at Ngapaeruru near Dannevirke in 1900. They also had an ingenious hoisting system for slinging logs across a ravine, which was illustrated and described in the *Auckland Weekly News* of 2 November 1900.

Henderson & Wratt, Dannevirke

These sawmillers had a tramway leading to their busy mill at Dannevirke in 1885.

H. Wilding & Co. Ltd, Waipukurau

This firm of timber merchants operated a large mill alongside the Waipukurau railway station and employed 17 men. The mill was connected to the NZR by a siding 12½ chains in length, and had a further 44 chains of tramway within the mill site, 9½ chains of which was used exclusively for the Napier-Hastings firewood traffic. The proprietors railed logs from the bush to the mill, and the average output of sawn timber was 130 000 feet per month.

The Waipawa Mail of Tuesday 10 March 1885, had an account of the company's truss tramway bridge near Takapau, which collapsed immediately after the passage of a loaded trolley. The horses and driver remained on the bank, but the trolley and logs rolled back into the creek. The accident was observed from a passing train. By employing four additional hands, the bridge was replaced in a few days.

Robert Holt & Sons Ltd, Napier

It is also known that this firm had a tramway at Piripiri at the turn of the century (1899). Piripiri station, which was situated between Mangatera and Matamau, has long since been closed.

Bartholomew Bros., Feilding

A lease to erect loading skids with tramway access at Matamau (41 mile peg) was granted to Bartholomew Bros. on 1 April 1901.

Gardner & Yeoman Ltd, Wakarara

Messrs Gardner & Yeoman had a wooden tramway leading from their Makarora mill near Wakarara, in the vicinity of the headwaters of the Waipawa River. It extended about two miles into the bush and was worked by horses, but was closed about 1943.

Hawke's Bay Timber Co., Puketitiri

A Lands & Survey Department's map of the Puketitiri area shows two tramways in that area. It is known that two miles of tramways were built in that area by the Hawke's Bay Timber Company as early as 1896, but very little is known of these lines, although it is presumed that tractors were used in later years.

Fraser & Son and Napier Timber Co., Willow Flat

There was at least one horse tramway used in the Maungataniwha area west of Kotemaori on the Willow Flat Road during the 1930s. There were two mills in this area, known as the top and bottom mills. They were operated by Fraser & Son, and by the Napier Timber Co., and both could have had tramways.

Hastings City Council Submarine Sewer Outfall, East Clive

Opened in March 1979 and closed in January 1981, this two-kilometre launching track was laid along Richmond Road from Mill Road to the highwater mark. Designed by Hastings City Council engineers and constructed by McConnell-Dowell Constructors Ltd, the track was laid in rails of 70 pounds per yard (35 kg/m) to a gauge of 3 feet 6 inches (1067 mm) on treated pine sleepers on a 200 mm thick bed of graded shingle ballast.

Ex-NZR bogies, mainly of types X25330, X25467 and X25830 with brake-gear removed and wooden pipe cradles added, were used to support pipe strings 1000 metres long, each constructed of prestressed concrete units 2.4 metres long with flexible joints to facilitate launching, during which the bogies were removed by dragline as they fell away from the pipeline into the recovery pit.

Motive power on land was a D8 tractor, but during the three launchings, a 60-tonne winch on a barge anchored in Hawke Bay was used. The only specialised rolling stock was an air compressor mounted on a bogie and used to pressurize the pipe strings to 20 pounds per square inch, thus reducing their weight from 1800 tonnes on land to 50 tonnes in seawater.

Costing $140,000 (altered bogies $70,000, track $70,000), the line was finally lifted in

LEFT: Part of a string of sewer pipes mounted on ex-NZR bogies on a track laid along Richmond Road, Clive, ready for launching as part of the Hastings City Council's submarine sewer outfall project, photographed in 1980.

Photograph: A. B. Fordyce

PRIVATE RAILWAYS

March 1981, the rails being sold to the Hawke's Bay Catchment Board for riverbank protection piling, and the bogies to McConnell-Dowell Constructors Ltd. Some bogies were purchased by the National Federation of Rail Societies. (Contributed by A. B. Fordyce and based on information supplied by the project design engineer, A. K. Thomson, Assistant City Engineer, Hastings.)

WHAT MIGHT HAVE BEEN

(Contributed by A. B. Fordyce)

TWO lines which never eventuated, but had they done so might well have changed the face of the Heretaunga Plains considerably, were both floated as private companies, although the projects eventually lapsed. Relevant material about these early lines in Hawke's Bay is not easy to find, and their inclusion here may well stimulate further research.

Some confusion exists as to whether there was more than one private company floated to bring the benefit of tramways to the area in the middle 1880s. Apparently the "City of Napier and Suburban Tramways Company" was formed in 1886 with a capital of £15 000 and H. S. Tiffen as Chairman. This company was to build a tramway between Napier and Taradale to a gauge of 2 feet 8 inches (813 mm), and a concession was granted to the company to lay tramlines in December 1886. H. S. Tiffen was a surveyor who owned extensive land holdings in the Jerviston area (modern-day Greenmeadows), and it is intriguing to find on a plan of Greenmeadows suburban and rural sections, which were auctioned on behalf of H. S. Tiffen on 13 October 1885, the route of a "proposed tramway to Hastings" along a line west of Pirimai creek, and roughly parallel with Tannery Road. The *H. B. Herald* of 6 October 1885 mentioned that the tramway "must pass in a direct line by Jerviston". In view of this, it is confusing also to find references to a "Taradale Tramway Company" registered in January 1887 and also having H. S. Tiffen as Chairman.

Whichever tramway actually had dealings with the local authorities, it is recorded that at first there was strong opposition but the roading authority later reversed its views and requested that, wherever a tramway was laid, the road width be increased by one third. A tramway would have been a logical alternative to the toll road which wound its way along the higher spots across the tidal salt marshes between Napier and Taradale, but consideration of costs, and the feeling that the time was not appropriate for such a work, led to the scheme's abandonment.

A much more grandiose project had been promoted in 1879. In the debate which raged in the late 1870s and the early 1880s over the formation of the Breakwater Port, some farmers and businessmen were at odds with the majority who, in 1885, voted to construct the port at its present location. Consequently, a company was formed under the title of the "Clive Grange Estate and Railway Company" to build an alternative port in the shelter of Cape Kidnappers between the Black Reef and Clifton. From Clive, a railway to be built at a cost of £3000 per mile would have crossed the Tukituki river on a combined road/rail bridge costing £10,000, to gain access to a concrete pier 2500 feet in length with double railway lines and craneway all costing £60,000. It was also intended to subdivide 600 acres of land to form a town, while 1100 acres of suburban land were to be allotted together with 3000 acres of small holdings, all of this to be situated on the Clive Grange Estate.

This estate was the property of Major-General the Hon. Sir George Stoddart Whitmore, K.C.M.G., who had purchased it in June 1873 after selling his property at Rissington. Whitmore was a member of the eleven-man Board of Directors, which included prominent names such as John Chambers of Te Mata, J. N. Williams of Frimley, John Harding of Mt. Vernon, the Hon. H. R. Russell of Waipukurau, and John Studholme of Christchurch. Upon Whitmore agreeing to sell the land to the company, for which they had budgeted £60,000, a prospectus was issued in April 1879 promoting the idea, with a capital of £75,000 in 1500 shares of £50 each. However, in May 1879, the project fell through, and the prospectus was withdrawn "due to the unfavourable monetary condition in the colony" at the time.

Did the promoters fall on hard times, or get cold feet, or was the opposition too great or the time just not right? We shall never be quite certain. With no more certainty can we envisage the Heretaunga Plains today, with the beach resorts of Haumoana and Te Awanga submerged in the city of "Clive Grange" and its attendant port of "Clifton".

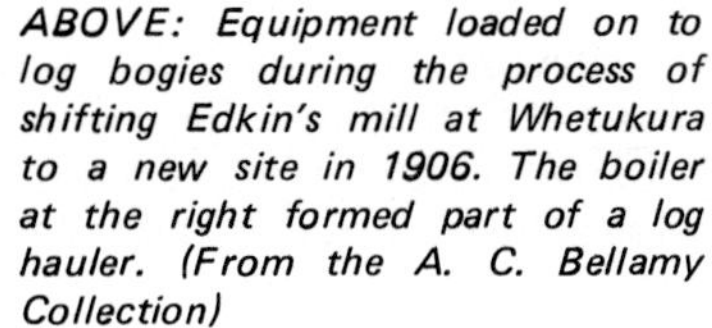

ABOVE: Equipment loaded on to log bogies during the process of shifting Edkin's mill at Whetukura to a new site in 1906. The boiler at the right formed part of a log hauler. (From the A. C. Bellamy Collection)

LEFT, UPPER: Horses and men have a rest during the haulage of logs along a tramway in the Maungataniwha area, Willow Flat, west of Kotemaori (north of Napier). (From the A. C. Bellamy Collection)

LEFT, LOWER: Six horses stir up the dust as they drag a log up what appears to be quite a steep gradient on a bush tram in the Umutaoroa district, north of Tahoraiti (see page 4). (From the A. C. Bellamy Collection)

ON THE BACK COVER: The Ruston Hornsby "DE165" class diesel-electric locomotive shunting the East Coast Farmers Fertilizer Company's works at Awatoto on 6 August 1979. (Photograph: E. C. G. Fletcher)

PRIVATE RAILWAYS